Favorite Pets

Guinea Pigs

by Christina Leaf

BLASTOFF!
Beginners

BELLWETHER MEDIA
MINNEAPOLIS, MN

Blastoff! Beginners are developed by literacy experts and educators to meet the needs of early readers. These engaging informational texts support young children as they begin reading about their world. Through simple language and high frequency words paired with crisp, colorful photos, Blastoff! Beginners launch young readers into the universe of independent reading.

Blastoff! Universe ★

Reading Level — Grade K — Grades 1-3 — Grade 4

Sight Words in This Book 🔍

a	have	on	to
are	in	the	up
do	it	their	want
eat	like	there	you
find	make	they	
good	many	this	

This edition first published in 2021 by Bellwether Media, Inc.

No part of this publication may be reproduced in whole or in part without written permission of the publisher. For information regarding permission, write to Bellwether Media, Inc., Attention: Permissions Department, 6012 Blue Circle Drive, Minnetonka, MN 55343.

Library of Congress Cataloging-in-Publication Data

Names: Leaf, Christina, author.
Title: Guinea pigs / by Christina Leaf.
Description: Minneapolis, MN : Bellwether Media, Inc., 2021. | Series: Favorite pets |
   Includes bibliographical references and index. | Audience: Grades K-1
Identifiers: LCCN 2020007101 (print) | LCCN 2020007102 (ebook) | ISBN 9781644873175 (library binding) |
   ISBN 9781681038049 (paperback) | ISBN 9781681037806 (ebook)
Subjects: LCSH: Guinea pigs--Juvenile literature. | Pets--Juvenile literature.
Classification: LCC SF401.G85 L43 2021 (print) | LCC SF401.G85 (ebook) | DDC 636.935/92--dc23
LC record available at https://lccn.loc.gov/2020007101
LC ebook record available at https://lccn.loc.gov/2020007102

Editor: Amy McDonald   Designer: Jeffrey Kollock

Printed in the United States of America, North Mankato, MN.

Table of Contents

Pet Guinea Pigs!

Do you want
a cuddly pet?
Guinea pigs are
a good pick!

Guinea pigs have soft fur. There are many kinds.

crested

American

Peruvian

7

Care

Guinea pigs live in cages. **Owners** wash the cages.

cage

owner

Guinea pigs
eat hay.
Apples are
a treat!

apple

hay

Owners brush
guinea pigs.
This makes
their fur soft.

brushing

Life with Guinea Pigs

Guinea pigs **chew** on toys. It keeps their teeth short.

teeth

chewing

Guinea pigs hide.
They find
safe spots.

Guinea pigs talk!
They **chirp**.
They purr.

chirping

Guinea pigs like to have friends. Buddy up!

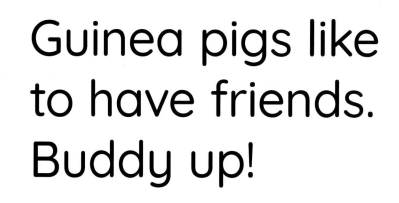

Guinea Pig Facts

Pet Guinea Pig Supplies

cage

spot to hide

food dish

Guinea Pig Toys

tunnel

chew toy

ramp

Glossary

chew

to bite with teeth

chirp

to make a short, sharp sound

owners

people who care for guinea pigs

To Learn More

ON THE WEB

FACTSURFER

Factsurfer.com gives you a safe, fun way to find more information.

1. Go to www.factsurfer.com.

2. Enter "pet guinea pigs" into the search box and click Q.

3. Select your book cover to see a list of related content.

Index